THE SWAN MACHINE

DEAN PARKIN

THE RIALTO

ACKNOWLEDGEMENTS

Some of these poems first appeared in the pamphlets *Irresistible to Women* (Garlic Press, 2003), *Just Our Luck* (Garlic Press, 2008), *The Sunshine of Fortune* (Xceptional Productions, 2013).

Acknowledgements are also made to the editors of the following publications in which the other poems first appeared: *Boomerang, Forward Book of Poetry 2003, Greensbro Review, The North, Prop, Reactions, The Rialto, Smiths Knoll* and *Smoke*.

I am indebted to so many people who have given energy and time, expertise and affection to the creation of these poems over the last twenty years. Thank you to each and every one of you. Finally, I am deeply grateful to Michael Mackmin for making this book happen.

First Published in 2016

The Rialto, PO Box 309, Aylsham, Norwich, England NR11 6LN

ISBN 978-1-909632-04-2

Dean Parkin and The Rialto gratefully acknowledge the contributions of the Subscribers, listed on page 64, who have made this publication possible.

The publisher also acknowledges financial assistance from Grants for the Arts.

The Rialto is a Registered Charity No. 297553
Typeset in Berling Roman 10pt on 12.5pt leading
Art Direction and Design by Starfish Norwich
Cover image by Annabel Dover
Printed in England by Page Bros, Norwich, Norfolk
Back cover photo: Katie Utting

LOTTERY FUNDED

For Michael Laskey and Naomi Jaffa

CONTENTS

THE SWAN MACHINE

lived in the kitchen, next to the fridge. Two feet high,
a black frame with a motor and drill for making
six holes in swans (three each side)
for daffodils to grow through. The plastic shavings
flew everywhere. My mother drilled
and turned up the radio. We kept the kitchen door shut.
My father stocked the garage with black sacks,
the occasional beak pecking through.
My mother drilled – each time she switched on,
the living room lights would flicker. When we heard
the drill skid and snarl, the machine would stop
and we knew she'd missed a hole and hoped
it was the swan that had taken the gouge. She sat
on one of our dining room chairs (covered,
so it wouldn't spoil). For comfort
there was a length of foam to rest her elbows on
as she held the swan up to the drill. She swore
when the dog wanted to be let out,
let back in, *Bloody dog!* The motor was slow
to start, rising to a whirr through the house.
She drilled to get cash from my father
who gave her more swans
and arthritis. *What's that?*
my friends would ask when the buzzing
interfered with Tomorrow's World.
That's my mother, I would say, proud
to have a swan machine in the house.

FATHER VALENTINE

was my mother, like her mother before her.
A local custom, beside the flowers and cards
with hearts, a sort of teatime Santa who interrupted
freezing February. The brown coat was bear-like,
the wellingtons weren't the best for running in,
the stocking over the head just plain disturbing –
and topped off by an old wig, matted. Did she change
in the garage after she made her excuses? *Just popping out
to the postbox. Just off to see Mrs East.* Not long before
a knock from the back door. No-one there
but slumped on the step, a bag with a string attached
leading to nothing but blackness. I reached down
(guessing sweets) but each time I tried to grab hold
the bag was tugged from my hand. I followed
until the string went slack, the prize
at my feet. Once we came face to face
when she leapt from behind the shed, *Boo!*
Word spread and long after my childhood,
she'd dig out the wig for other kids in the village.
The year she stopped she blamed the boys –
grown up too quick. Not satisfied
with a marshmallow cone or liquorice stick.

THE WAITING ROOM

The story of the nut allergy. How you know you've got it
and why you aren't dead. The story of the whelk
stuck in your throat, of the fishing line hooking
Simon King by the cheek. The story of the kipper
and the grandmother, my mother's story,
the story I always get wrong. *You just make things up!*
The story of the father and two sons in search of the cat –
each brought back a different one – and the story
of the real cat, which came back while they were out looking.
The story of watching the morning arrive,
the sky clicking on its light, like that. And the three men
on a lawn massaging someone else's girlfriend until
that light came on. Like your story of the two of you,
taking off your clothes, lying there together,
just talking, not remembering touching.
The story of the woman on the bus, of how beautiful
a woman can be, surrounded by pensioners and a young man
with tremendous acne. The story of the warts, of the place
on your finger where you can still feel you had them.
The story of it being thirty years ago, of filling milk bottles
with lemon squash. The story of the stock car race, of the flag
I bought there, the orange it was and the rust
that made its flagpole brown. The story of running,
how it's not a race any more, of getting older. Realising it's not
going to stop until it does. The story of the waiting room,
of having nothing to read, of thinking to yourself
how long am I going to be? The story of seventeen seconds
one afternoon when you wanted to change
everything, then decided against it. The story of nothing
but the same old story, the long story
you were told to cut. *Get to the bloody point!*

LUCK

Because you should not see it through glass
Auntie Sylvia would phone to warn us
the new moon was out.
My mum would be on her feet –
Where's my blasted purse? – and gone,
letting in the cold, slippers in the yard,
ten pence piece in her hand to turn
so she'd be lucky. I must have been thirteen
by the time I asked about her specs,
aren't they glass? *Of course!*
she said. *That's why!* All those years
turning silver for nothing. Even now
with glasses off, she's outside still looking
though she must know her coin's
more nickel than precious metal.
If the moon can't be seen – *Damn cloud!* –
she'll turn it over anyway, last month she did.
Scratch card next day, fifty quid.

FRENCH LESSON

When the family were absent
and unaccounted for
his older sister's friend
was teaching him French,
pomme is apple,
pomme de terre is potato,
an apple in the earth
she laughed. Uninterested,
he decorated paper with doodles.
She started to talk
about school teachers
he would come up against,
still talking
as she casually shed
the yellow floral print dress.
He couldn't remember any knickers
but there was a bra
she disconnected from her back
before untying her ginger hair.
Don't be afraid of your body,
she said and his eyes were drawn
suddenly over so much skin
that he could only think pink,
and though he often tried to recall more
it was only her face he could focus upon,
a face he found years later, now almost
hidden in this woman
spilling out of a vest and shorts,
cawing children flapping about her,
giving herself
to an ice-cream, a strawberry one,
melting fast.

PERFECTLY GOOD REASON

Me, as a kid, retreating to the outside loo to discover
new countries and oceans in the cracked paint on the walls.
My sister sent to fetch me again, to find out if I'm okay.

The navel fluff collection in the eggcup on the mantlepiece.
The toaster I forgot on the lawn, where I threw it
during the second wave of the attack of the ants.

I can always blame my father. He never sent postcards
but did bring us back napkins and sugar sachets
from the airport cafés of Tunisia and Crete.

My mother kept busy, baking a shepherd's pie each Monday
before Mrs Myall finally pleaded *please, no more –
I've been vegetarian for years.*

Today it's my landlord as I explain the forest of beer bottles
growing out of the sink on their way to the bottle bank.
The reason why the washing-up is shoved in the oven.

NUMBER 32

I'll leave the thumb print in the artex but remake two rooms
with a dividing wall, restore the hearth, nurse a fire,
Nanny Jessie's chair in the corner, dressing gown on the door.

Upstairs I'll put two record players, the summer
of Jackson Browne in one bedroom, Twisted Sister in the other.
In the bathroom I place the all-in-one toilet roll holder and ashtray.

In the kitchen here's the pantry, the back door returned to where
it should be. I swap white dresser for formica, potato masher
ready to drum on the ceiling calling us down for tea.

Across the beams of the garage, his golf clubs where he left them.
Against the wall where we stood I'll guess our heights with chalk,
won't throw down my Grifter but lean it neatly on the other bikes.

In the yard, I resurrect the coal bunker, its only ever use
for football and a quick one-two. I drag back the long gate
and shut it gently, where Kristy waits behind it three dogs ago.

Lastly I repaint the house blue, 1970s style, so we can see it for miles
across fields and even from here. Climb the hill that gets steeper
until I'm standing to pedal, pushing harder to get back.

MY FATHER'S HAIR

From the 50s quiff with the Brylcreem bounce
to the post-Beatles fringe and parting, blow-waved
and sprayed in the 70s, gelled in the 80s,
my father still had his long after mine
and its early departure. Took a pride in his visits to Mick's
Cutting Crew; a man of sixty, still a natural brown.
He often wondered where I got my hair cut
and were they both trimmed at the same time? Reasoned
it must be my brains coming out the top of my head.
He approached retirement with a flicker of white
he tried to hide by keeping it short
at the sides with the beginnings of a thinning
spiral at his crown I was always quick to point out.
By the time all I could do for him
was cancel the appointment (Mick said he was sorry
and I was sorry too for ringing so late) it was the only thing
that was recognisably him. Longer
than he'd have liked, licked back
by a flannel, flattened
against a pillow the last time I saw him,
the first time I touched my father's hair.

PRESENT

Lurking at the end of the asbestos garage
behind a stack
of umpteen ancient paint tins
beneath the cobwebbed
workbench ruins
and one hard roll of lino –
my go-kart. A present
from dad, shiny bright red
it was, with black taped stripes.
I was never off it,
trundling for miles up and down the yard,
sending Billy-next-door berserk.
I bring it out into the sunshine
of a different century, it's faded grey
and I try to wipe away the dust.
It wasn't ever new, my oldest sister chips in,
he resprayed it. Cheapskate.
I squeeze into the seat,
fold my legs, push my feet
into the stiff rusted pedals.
She takes a picture.

It's a short ride
and one day it's down to you –
I don't want this you say
but it's yours, you have to
pick the damn thing up
with both hands, steady yourself,
throw it away.

THE LOKE

You went down it, *I'm taking the dog*
down the loke, a different walk
for when it looked like rain
or you didn't want to come across the other kids.
It was sheltered by a straggling line of trees
which divided two fields, Bibbler Boon's
on your left and on your right Mr Bennett's,
where on the furthest corner
lay buckled corrugated iron, the charred remains
of the old Isolation Hospital. It was during the war,
my mother told me, sickly soldiers made this journey
down the track, a bumpy ride, laid up
in an ambulance. She told me enough
not to want to go near, so I could scare myself
when I'd gone too far down the loke, dawdling
until dusk was all shadow
and the rain-peppered puddles shook –
suddenly I wasn't going to make it back
before dark, turning for home,
boy and little dog.

BUGGERLUGS

School was a joke for you, Bugsy,
like inking the four corners
of Stephen Hamble's rubber
and waiting for the blue
to invade his map of Europe.
I laughed, but later
you were less appreciated,
when the rest of the kids grew
serious, started working,
revising for O's and A's.
Some teacher you were lippy to
barked back, *If you want to be*
a petrol pump attendant all your life
you're going the right way about it.
But you knew of a job laying pipes
in Jo'burg, where the real dosh was,
could afford to scoff at Paul
sending off to the G.P.O.
and Eggy at the 'leccie company
like his Dad. Last time we spoke
you were *Outta here*, on your bike
with the handlebars turned
the wrong way. You passed
the school bus and I watched you
not stopping for the red light,
up the pavement and cutting through
the Shell garage, then
back on the road again,
freewheeling, no hands.

JIMMIE SULPHUR IN THE STARLIGHT

No-one wanted to know where I was going
but I wanted to be asked so I could tell them
I was meeting Jimmie Sulphur in the Starlight –
the café, me nursing a sausage roll till closing-time.
How can you eat that shit? he'd say. My mother said
Sulphur can't be his real name and he can't even spell Jimmy
properly. We were eighteen in 1988 and no good
at being this young, nostalgic for another time
still to come. Jimmie was the only man in town
to persist with a parting and to shave each day
in the face of designer stubble. He could kick
a ball up onto his shoulders, roll it down his back
and flick it with his heel over his head. He didn't,
not any more, not with his glasses. We had wheels now –
but only on alternate weekends and Thursdays
when Pod's dad wasn't working – a Lada estate in cream,
automatic, that took us round the ring road and back
to another Saturday night ending on the sea wall.
We'll get piles sitting here, I said. Piles of what? he said.
We're cold, Pod said, our goosebumps have goosebumps.
You can go, he said, where you gonna go? The girls
we wanted would never find us here. Local girls,
he said, don't bother with them, they don't bother me.
We wanted to climb the rocks but the danger signs
seemed sensible. We used the cigarettes in the glove box
to burst the yellow and blue balloons celebrating
25 years of Clives' Quality Cars. Why are we doing this?
asked Pod. Because Clive's got nothing to celebrate,
he replied, and doesn't know where to shove his apostrophe.
We felt like the last boys in town until we met the late night
lads in Paradise Kebabs who laughed at anything

and especially Jimmie who, because he didn't look
like them, and because he stood, back turned to them,
got a squeezy bottle of mayonnaise squirted down his neck,
his glasses sent flying. Ending up on the floor, he looked
somehow less complicated. Back on the sea wall
I said something or other about the stars, wondering
what they meant. Pod said his watch must be broken,
the time was wrong. Right, said Jimmie, let's go.

LONE WOLF

Back on a bench in the bus shelter or what's left – one side no glass,
        kicked in, the other cracked –
my snooker cue case is the clue I've been with friends this evening,
        I don't play this game alone.
Buster and Smurf are just lucky to live in town, already home by now
        and I'm trying to think
of the frames, my own fluke break of 27, my best ever (I lied about
        the 42 I got playing my old man).
My breath is all clouds, my teeth chatter, I pull up my collar.
        That jacket this weather? my mum said.

I'm trying not to think what happened here last week and the girls
        who want to sit where I'm sat,
whipped up on some joke, the punchline *How many you had?*
        they take turns repeating.
The one called Cat asks me for a light. There are better answers
        than I don't smoke actually
which gets *What do you do? And how much you charge?* Ending with
        Your name Happy Harry?
Or the week before and the slow car that goes past, brakes and waits
        not far down the road, engine running.

Or the comeback of Fat and Thin. Fat trailing, Thin spots me
        and diverts to the shelter.
Cold, he says, half a question. *Out with your pool stick?* Silence
        joins us on the bench.
You had a good night? We've not, my friend. Nowhere to stay.
        I dig into my pocket. He backs off
to a street light to count, slowly. *Nah, that's not enough*, he says.
        You got anywhere? A sofa? A floor?
Fat picks at his nails, pulls out something sharp to scrape out dirt.
        This your bus? You got to go?

So, it's a relief when tonight this one man walks up. Dressed for it,
      all winter hat, coat and gloves.
Keeps himself to himself, stands out of the shelter, like he's got a sign
      'Do Not Disturb' round his neck.
And here's the thing, he doesn't get on when it arrives. I want to
      tell him *This is the last bus, mate,*
but can't. Lone Wolf, I think, as I watch him taking my place
      on the bench, me
huddled up on a seat on the bus, chin pushed down in my jacket,
      home before I know it.

TANDEM

They meet – the jogger going down the gentle hill,
on the way up a woman and boy on a bicycle, purpose built
for mother and child (the seat is lower at the back).
The road is a one lane track, a parting between
plush fields. On the bank to let them by the grass kicks up wet,
still fresh. She's a hippie mum – the jogger remembers
her as red, she wore red, a summer dress over scarlet leggings,
bunches tied with ribbons. Even her glasses tinted.
He's a typical schoolboy, growing into his royal blue sweater,
beetling away, pedalling as if chasing, never to catch up.
The boy might recall all this, or a detail or two, perhaps
the lightning tree or the barn with a roof and straw bale walls.
He will take his own picture – the downpour (drenched
they turned back, laughing). Or the day of the piglet escape,
the postman and cross tractor driver waiting to pounce
as it zigzagged between them. And the jogger will remember this
as the summer he tried to get fit only to realise that running
just makes it seem like you live longer. How far to go
or where to turn back? A quick smile,
as they pass, exchange a small good morning.

BUG FLY GNAT

you can't tell for sure, but your paths crossed,
you do know that, the tiny insect appeared
at the right moment with the exact trajectory
to enter straight into your mouth and hit
the back of your throat with what, if it were aiming,
would have been *the* perfect shot, at such a speed
that closing your mouth was not only too late
but acted like the doors of a trap snapped shut
with pleasure at your catch. And then your own body
kicks in with the necessary saliva, the automatic
swallow before finally the brain revolts
and provides reaction: you cough, splutter, speak
words not found in the dictionary – *Eeerrk, Carghhh*.
It was a fluke, fate, a union meant to be.
Look, you should not have been there,
questions will be asked about why
you were absent from your stacked desk,
why you were out walking (you do not
go for walks) down a lane, scouting
round hedgerows (this is not one of your pastimes).
Just luck then, but not for the bug – killed
and digested, an unfortunate destiny fulfilled.
And you have to turn another corner, your mouth
open wider than ever at the morning's impact,
when straight towards you, at a precise angle,
come two sprint cyclists and an excitable horse.

THE COBBLER LAUREATE

26,000 copies. Twenty-six thousand
sold within two years, *The Farmer's Boy*
by Robert Bloomfield, Suffolk-born
self-taught peasant poet. *Blum*-field.
Too weak to work on the land, he left

for London to learn a trade and wrote
the verse that made his name. Hero to John Clare
who treasured a scrap of his handwriting,
to Byron he was *The Cobbler Laureate*
whose success robbed us of a great shoemaker.

Poor Bob. He couldn't forget his poverty, writing
to his brother George, *The sunshine of fortune*
may require an umbrella. And the downpour
was constant. He buried a daughter,
his family exploited his kindness, his wife

gave their money to a religious sect, his publisher
went bust, his income dried up, his health (never good)
grew worse – headaches, rheumatism, eyesight
failing. His words though, hammered out
in the rhythms and din of the workshop

were read for a century or more,
became poems people found on their tongue,
recited from, memorised reams – lines
he had given his mind to, carried in his head
until he could nail them down for good.

THE FAMILY PORTRAIT
After the paintings of Harry Becker

It's the face you can't see I recognise –
cap pulled down, big lugs, roll-up
bobbing on his bottom lip. Jack's alive

in every painting – the young version
of the old man I knew, animated again,
treading the earth under oversized boots.

I could add his barley water bottle of cold tea,
the orange twine, teeth for special occasions –
Wunt have em in for goin t'work!

After Becker, after horses, Jack had nothing
but the land, had no truck with tractors, stuck
to hoeing, hedging, ditching, then

an allotment down our garden, our shed
was his. I broke into crusted tobacco tins
for the magic pink runner bean seeds.

Permanent he seemed – like the heavy iron roller
corroded, stalled in a corner, like the age
he took to chuck a sprout stalk on the heap.

HEAD HORSEMAN
For my great grandfather (1969–1923)

Not the stern family portrait
with Alice, his church-going wife
and four children. The other photo –
just him with the Shire horse
is as close as I'll get to his smile.

We know that she was trouble
(an accident, a man killed)
enough so that a picture of this mare
at ease was something rare, worth catching.
He was the only one who could handle her –

John William Wilson, father unknown,
mother, Mary Ann, a milkmaid, dead at 25.
Brought up by his grandfather (who died),
his uncle (who died), his aunt who re-married
a thief who was jailed. From bare-knuckle boxer

to head horseman, a man of few words
but we do know his last, from his sick bed
growled at the parson, sent for by his wife –
I dunt wunt to see no sky pilot.
Thirty years a widow, she never spoke of him.

With him gone though
they could do nothing with the horse
but sell her. It was something about his calm
hand on the bridle, the other gentle on the shoulder
that steadied her down.

TRAP

September pretending to be summer,
I escape on my bike, glad to get lost
to find this farm – the straw baled, barns full
of quiet. Not a soul, like the rapture.

I pedal on, around another field
and the next turn I see them – three cages
each with a bird. I hope not alive but one by one
they hop and twitch, captives in black. Rooks.

The first backs away as I get closer. A pet
you might have thought – metal bowl for water,
plate of seeds. But I knew it was a trap.
The second eyed me sideways, could tell

I was no good. By the third cage I had to stop.
Expert construction of wire, a puzzle to open.
The farmhouse so near, all windows.
Or the gamekeeper in the cover of the trees.

None of your business, I hear them say, me
still a boy, them the old men, country people
in the village, the long dead, the distant
relatives, farm workers, grown-ups, my mother.

The yellow sun glares. Best be on my way –
unsteady on the rough stubble, unable
to ride the bike, afraid
even to glance back.

ROOTED

Pleased to be free
of the family occupation –
ag lab, ag lab, ag lab
one census to the next
crosses for signatures
unmarked graves.
Peasants. Hard old lives.
A printer's compositor
may have escaped
but even my uncle
was a cowman.
University not for us.
Though I know
a few long words
I left school at sixteen
can't name tree or bird
the countryside something
you drive through.
Escaped but not gone far
still here, just
part of the scenery
I'm at home with
that's grown on me.

THE RENEGADE ASTRONOMER'S GUIDE
TO OUR WORLD & BEYOND

Not exactly what I was looking for
jammed in a tight bottom shelf
alongside an ancient London A to Z,
undisturbed for the dozen or so years since
it arrived in a box of odds and ends
I might like. *Bloody amazing book!*
I hear him say, never so thrilled by anything
I'd ever given him. I could read it,
like spending an afternoon with him, but won't
get to see him pause, envelope as bookmark,
chapters still to go. *Now*, he'd say,
I know what I was going to tell you.

QUIET ROAD HOME

We haven't spoken for miles and I nearly let it pass
but I want to go back, so turn around in a sudden side road,
a quick shift that squeals wheels, try to explain, *I need
to show you*. You're unsure what's been said but won't ask.

We've gone further than I thought, the road winding
up hills I can't recall coming down, one sharp corner
after another, the day greyer, the drizzle, drab October.
Then, there it is, between trunk, bramble, hedge: pumpkins.

A pumpkin patch. And a trailer-full, a bubbling mass
of glowing orange. For the farmer perhaps it's just work –
bend and lift – but we agree it's a kids' picture book,
a happy ending. We turn around, talk. It's the talking I miss.

ON HOPE

I was hoping you would come and find me.
That the door would open and you would push it
beyond the snag of the carpet and throw in light
from the landing. You might say my name, as a question,
before you edge on to this bed. That you would be hoping
I would be here is perhaps too much to hope for,
that you would want, now, to be at my side.
I know the stairs are a long way to travel. I hear
the flow of conversation, spurts of laughter,
and of course you are immersed, the hostess,
in kitchen, dining or living room, you can't be
absent, there are demands, but I was hoping you would
notice I wasn't there, guess, come and find me.
I have walked out on small talk and can't step back.
Our eyes have not met all evening. You are annoyed,
I am angry, so I was hoping you might join me
in this spare room and not need
to say anything, we won't have to speak,
instead you would slide onto this bed
beside me, we would settle and eventually
touch, that would be enough, I hope, to touch.

LEMON TREE, THREE FEET TALL,
TO BE CARRIED ACROSS LONDON

with a single sample of full grown fruit that hangs precarious
from its lowest branch.
Yellowing
hand grenade, solo bauble, dangly earring, citric scrotum,
an only child sleeping,
rocking,
that slender stem.
On the 15.23, they'll arrive right on time for rush hour,
dumped on platform nine
to navigate the station, the jostle, the tube, down escalators
and up eventually to the street and *Taxi! Taxi!*
All that lies ahead
but they have got this far –
the safety of the train. And the tree is healthy, perky,
leaves not shedding.
An unlikely tourist then, natural and strange
among the plastic and vinyl of the carriage.
Next to the tree, the right man for the task. Confident,
nonchalant, young enough,
he thumbs a paperback.
The stalk is sturdy, he must think.
I want him to get home tall, cargo intact
not pathetic
and explaining, *This was on there, like that.*
I want him to get there, please –
whether it be mother or lover, she hears the gate
expecting him of course,
surprised therefore
by the bell,
by what he brings. *For you* he says,
this tree and lemon he knew she would love.

SWEET OFFER

Do you want a murray mint? I ask.
Not the best place, the beach, at night
in November – *bracing* you call it, wind
smattered with rain – as deep in my pocket
my fingers recover one of last summer's
half-melted sweets. Further down the shore

you tell me what you thought I'd said:
Do you want to marry me? How I continued
It might be a bit sticky, and then
I'm not selling this to you, am I? as I fudged
in my jacket for the something I held out
and pressed into your palm.

THE PIGEON EXPLODED

gripped tail first by the slow truck's front wheel, trapped
then pop and confetti
of feather and ketchup in full view
of two young people
who embrace against the short horror show.
Her face pushed into his chest, the black T-shirt
won't wipe away what she just saw
but does give somewhere for tears
to run. This couple, if we can call them that,
forget last night, the bad month
(she said it started last March), him soothing her,
It was an old pigeon, it was an ill pigeon as if
he had been watching the last shambling steps. Knowing
her history, he connects this naturally
with her father and the house martin's eggs,
so tries holding her again
gently. Perhaps they can forget the sentence
about wanting children
but certainly not with you.
She keeps on crying though
because it's dead and gross and tears
seem easier now and the truck should have stopped
while he says nothing because it will pass
and they both know
that not even exploding pigeons
can hold them together for long.

THE FAMILY SHOPPING

The girl joins Mum in the bookshop, says Dad wants her opinion
          next door, a jacket he likes.
Mum says, no, tell him I'm not interested, but the girl wants her to
          come because he'll only ask her
what she thinks then and how does she know? So she stays there
          pleading, go on Mum, please go,
until he arrives himself and explains. There are two he really likes,
          one's light and the other's a stiffer leather
but she says she doesn't know why he asks her about something
          she wouldn't dream of buying herself,
how you said *you* were coming to buy clothes and now you won't.
          It's your decision. It's up to you.
Looking for Aromatherapy, she leaves him picking at Local History
          before he circles round and tries again.
What about the style of the jacket then, can't you at least comment
          on that? But she won't relent,
says it's like Sophie asking if she should have purple hair or blue
          and Sophie agrees, adds you're like that
when Mum asks anything. You won't help me then, he asks weakly
          and repeats it, you won't help me.

WHITE SLICED LOAF

The big friendly blind lady and her cumbersome labrador
were impassable in the tight aisle
of the small town supermarket, so I held back,
faked interest in an Easter egg display
and could only watch as I was overtaken
by another woman heading straight for the bread, first noticing
the one-tone brown, stiff, shoulder-length wig
so when she turned I knew not to stare
though she had looked away, the large sunglasses half-hiding
her face, scarred and tissue-white, as her hand was touched
and held, a question boomed out,
Excuse me my darling, could you find me a white sliced loaf?
Her small surprised, *Yes*
of course – there's only one left. The unabashed response,
Thank you, you're ever so lovely.

THE LAST CUSTOMER

This one has nowhere to be
or if he has it's somewhere alone,
so you're his last contact of the day
and he's not letting go easily.
There's a book he wants ordered
if he could remember the title
or author, is it Mantripp, Manthorpe
or Longthorn, it might come back to him
and if it did could we order it?
Yes, another day perhaps,
but he's not finished yet, tries again,
goes through his shopping, shows me
the price of jam, two for one,
a bag of tangerines, reduced to this.
He'll be on his way now, he expects
I'll want to close, asking me for the time
as he backs off, retreats to the pavement.
Locking the door between him and me,
I wave, wish him goodnight through the glass,
when actually it's only late afternoon
and the whole evening looms ahead.

HOT DOG

The smell of hot dogs reminds him
how he used to like them, how long it's been
since he had one and with plenty of time,
five minutes to kill and five minutes
to get to the interview five minutes early,
he joins the queue. Orders a jumbo, agrees
to onions, foolishly adds brown sauce
which slips off the sausage and gathers
into a slick which starts to drip out of the roll,
dribbles over his cuff, onto his tie. The streaks
on his chin he smears with a tissue, spreads
to his cheek, even manages to rub on his forehead,
and with time escaping, as the last slither of onion
skids down his jacket, he has to run.
It's further than he thought but arriving late
he still has to wait, the secretary telling him
to sit, offering him a chair in the exact spot
where the sun cuts across the room. Left alone,
panting, pulling at his collar, sizzling in the heat,
he realises he smells of onions, finds his fingers
tainted with grease, just as the boss appears,
all smiles, to shake him by the hand.

BEGINNER'S GUIDE TO BODY LANGUAGE

On page 55 he found the legs section,
the way she crossed hers,
feet definitely turned towards him.

He remembered she had fiddled with her hair
and fingered her earrings, which he had blamed
on the awkward silence. Yet page 86

said these were good signs, her drawing attention
to herself. So pushing back her sleeves
was not because the room was stuffy,

but to expose the delicate skin on her wrist
which he had missed at the time and was sorry now.
For his part, next time they met, in the restaurant,

he tried to keep one hand in his pocket
(pointing in the obvious direction, page 89)
even when seated. Holding her gaze

a little longer than necessary (page 34)
was easy, especially when trying
to check out her unconscious pupil dilation.

Suggesting a starter, he imagined her
foot slipping in and out of its shoe,
like page 97 said it would, as he watched

her face, her pretty mouth opening,
closing, opening as she asked him again
Why is it you never seem to listen?

THIRD WISH

Lastly she wished for Bernard Turnbull,
her lecherous Sixth Form maths teacher,
to be irresistible to women. Granted,
a surprising choice, especially for Bernie,
now retired. At that moment he was shopping
in Tesco's with Olive, his wife of forty years,
when suddenly the girl behind the deli counter
unpopped her pink checked shirt, offering more
than his request for a slice of ox tongue. *Bloody women*,
he sighed, as they interrupted his slow progress home
to steal kisses or caress one of his chins, demanding
to slide fingers through his sparse greased hair.

Bernard had already lost his appetite
and at teatime pushed away his bread and butter
pudding, explaining he fancied an early night.
Calling to Olive not to forget his Ovaltine, he peeped
through the bedroom curtains at the cooing girls
gathering at his gate. Then Olive appeared
bulging in the door frame, clad in a sheer nightie
Bernard could only say looked chilly. She growled
at him, pinned him down to the bedspread, as he wished
for nothing more than his warm milk, his Wilbur Smith,
his hot water bottle, muttering about it being a sorry day
when a man didn't feel safe in his own pyjamas.

THE LANDING

She bought a crescent moon,
a wooden one with a friendly face,
and hung it at the top of the stairs.
He was enchanted,
imagined the whole sky,
giving her a sun, fixing it
to the opposite wall. He wondered
about the stars he could make for her
and he was pleased with them,
letting himself in to add another cluster
to the ceiling, while she pretended
not to notice or care until the morning
he arrived with black paint. Then she told him
he was leaving, put everything
in a box and handed it to him.
She needed her own space.

YEARNING FOR QUINCE

A dirty hog in the house is better than no hog
at all, my wife told me, ironing creases
into my boxer shorts, pressing them flat.

Since my house is burning, I thought to myself,
I may as well warm myself at it, watching Helen in the office,
my mind going further than the soft skin of her neck.

Do not dress in clothes made of leaves, I read somewhere,
when going to put out a fire, and I went home
two days later without any alibi or wanting one.

If you sleep with a dog, my wife shouted, you wake up
full of fleas, and the conversation continued between us
slamming doors until she finally changed the locks.

I have plenty of apples and pears, my father once told me,
but my heart yearns for quince and that I can understand,
as I close in on Helen's mother, unattended in reception.

A MAN SETS OFF EARLY FOR WORK

with every good intention but parking his car, catches his thumb
in the door handle, so it feels like the nail has been prised up
from its bed. He walks away, briefcase in one hand, the other hand
raised, thumb held up in disbelief as he waits at the kerb's edge.
A white sports car pulls up, the window slides down and a woman
asks where he is thumbing a lift to. *Go away*, he mumbles, words
half lost in his throat, and she, catching only the *away* part, opens
the door and the man, given the choice, gets in. He looks at her,
this woman, whom he would describe as plain if asked, as she asks
him his name and he decides to stop this, to get out, to go back.
Can I explain? he says but at that moment the woman changes gear
and the word explain is drowned beneath the thrum of the engine
and she only hears *Can I* which she takes as Kenny. Assuming
a new name, being driven without an idea of destination, the man
wonders about his wife and conjures up her face, wants to tell her
how much he loves her. *I love you* he says out loud for the first time
since he can remember and the woman swerves then slows down,
pulls into a layby, and says *We've only just met and this is crazy,
but I feel the same way.* Stop! he thinks, but is now too frightened
to open his mouth so says nothing, as she kisses him and kisses
him again and tells him about all the pain in life she has suffered,
does he know about pain? He nods as he remembers his thumb.

VELVET

he called her one day
as he moved his hand
across her thigh, said something stupid like
your skin is velvet,
and she loved it and the name stuck.
This was nothing to do with a dog he once knew.
No, no, nothing to do with the red setter called Velvet.
He tries to expel this from his mind
but the chestnut hair is the same though,
and she is thin like that dog was
and now you mention it, walks like it too,
sort of lopes, but he shouldn't think of her like that.
After all, Velvet was only some dog he used to take for walks
years ago, after school for pocket money.
Why don't we go for long walks any more?
she says, starts to beg, let's go for a walk by the sea,
but he just can't, tells her he feels a cold coming on.
She asks him if he wants her to fetch anything.
It was difficult now
to stroke her, you never make a fuss of me,
she says and lies back like she wants him
to rub her belly.
Honey, she says, you never call me Velvet now.
Don't you think I'm like Velvet?
I can't stop thinking about you, he says,
holding her in his eyes and it's true,
and he finds himself reaching out
to pat her on the head.

THE DIZZYING

At the end of town you'll find dusk and the circus,
an excuse to be out late for three boys
and one girl who is allowed because
she's someone's sister, though younger, still
a girl doing handstands so you can nearly see –
Did you see that! But it's colder now, too cold
for T-shirts and shorts and working out the next game
where they all take turns – *Spin around three times
then close your eyes.* We've all been this kind of dizzy
wanting now not to stop with its string of lights
and muffled drum roll. Then comes the moon
but on whose side? The sensible boy
walking his bicycle home or the girl leaving us
with one last cartwheel to distant final applause.

ARRIVING

On the 16.04 I'm surrounded by boy-men
in baggy shorts and white T-shirts,
school kids, talking fast
about bikes and c.c.s and Pug's sister
who rides her mum's moped
and she's not sixteen yet.
Two girls want to know how come the boys
got seats and they didn't and six volunteers say,
Sit here, you can sit here on my lap,
and one does while the other nudges past me
to the window seat opposite.
She admires the view, as if
she hadn't seen it before,
while the conversation swings from Adam
who's going to be six foot three
because his brother is, to the girl on the lap
who gets a laugh when she says
she can feel something
but not much. Ash has a massive blackhead –
My mum does mine for 50p each!
You must be a millionaire!
And Henry Reid is a werewolf, with hair
that thick on his chest
and back. His eyebrows meet,
explains Jamie, putting his finger on his own
proud gap, while Ryan's only got
a *few* hairs on his shoulders.
Kelly shaves her legs every day and Daniel
wears Y-fronts
(because they're *comfortable*)
and did anyone know that

there are three kinds of pubic hair –
black, brown, and ginger haired people have...
Ssshh, tell it to everyone I should!
Then the train began to slow
and as it tucked neatly into the station
they were ready by the doors
pounding the button marked Open.

LUNCH HOUR IN THE GRAVEYARD

Better the graveyard than most places, the leaves
get together to wish for a breeze and the church provides
tall shade. Gravestones grown wonky, the simplest
inscriptions buffed away – serif and curlicue –
anything ornate cracked or snapped off,
collapsing monuments, dog-eared tombs
lids banded with curling ivy. At least two stones,
names long gone, pleasingly joined as one,
say more than most. And I'm happy to be here
with this dressed-up decline and at the gate
an A-board – *Revival Antiques & Collectables* –
all peeling tape and paper that won't last longer
than this afternoon. I'm the only one around,
up to me, it seems, to clock the irrelevant passing –
a baby's babble, a moped beep, a woman
weighed down, all summer dress and bulging
shopping, a pigeon with one song
on a loop, a snippet of a helicopter clips
the corner of the sky but comes no closer.
And if ever there was a sign, a dragonfly
zips by. I know I am in the best place
to rest, this bench I can leave, take a deep breath
because I can, stretch so my feet lift,
loosen my shoulders and come back to life.

HERNIA

In the split second
between sitting and standing
I grew old one day.

You know the phrase 'long in the tooth'?
smiled the dentist
explaining the receding gums.

Struggling out of the chair
wondering what time it was
not getting to the phone.

*Should I leave this white hair
with the others?* asked the barber
overlooking my prematurely bald head.

Now up on my feet
squinting for my glasses, maintaining
I still have a boyish twinkle.

It's very common the young doctor said
with the onset of middle age
her hand definitely on my groin.

OLD ENOUGH TO BE YOUR DAUGHTER

Not moralising – simple
arithmetic. Her
tipsy, dropping in she's twenty
between hiccups. Me
with shirts suddenly older than her.

OTHER MEN

and men like me. Unlikely men, quiet men,
businessmen, broken men, park bench men,
the top ten handsome men to the two men in the pub,
men like the one you saw in the street.
The bogeymen we're told about at school
which some of us become. The what-happened-to-us men?
You know you can't trust us, like men with beards
a different shade from their hair, like married men, men with brains
in their pants which might mean any men –
in their cars, with their toys, in stereo, young again
men turn boy-racers when the light goes green.
Men versus men? With nothing better to do
than sit on a sofa and throw peanuts
to the other and catch them in their mouth. *One-nil!*
Men in late summer, spent in shorts and sandals,
baggy T-shirts coping with the belly spread.
Men dusting in pinafores, cleaning
their paw prints off light switches. Useless men
who can't change a fuse, won't budge an inch,
will never talk and *don't listen.* Grown men
behaving like big stubbly babies – the reason women,
teeth clenched, say *Men!* Still in their socks,
not washing up, men who suddenly fall over.
Attention men, stand up and be men, boys
becoming men, men who aren't as young
as they were, older men, who get the joke,
grown grey like old men still going strong, losing none
of their spark. Friends and gentlemen, good men,
men you're glad are there, spirits
like fires, to warm your hands by. *Amen.*

PASSER-BY

I was crossing a cemetery. A short cut
in a town I knew well but this route as new
as September, suddenly sunny, summer revived.

Vast rolling place, I could see no end,
the dead and their stones scattered in the green
among muddled paths that pointed to the exit.

I started counting the graves in my sight,
stopped at fifty, enough for a good crowd
and resurrected each one, stood them up –

grey men awoken, some expecting heaven,
young mothers and babies, a soldier, no age at all,
a boy really, reunited with his grown old wife

dusting themselves down, blinking
in the bright afternoon, they did not see me
as any different, only I could insist I was.

THE PROGRESS

The mess, the waste, the jumble, the endless
hassles and glitches, the phased or fizzled out,
the fretting, the punctured, the doubts, the anguish,
the entire dismal pug-ugly business. From this,
out of the front door,
a man. The morning still dark,
must be early or winter, but here he is
through the gate, from the wretched,
not exactly awake but a start,
showered, shaved and nicked, awoken
nobody, not yet spoken, relieved
at the slow progress – the milk float,
the zigzag of a paperboy
though the light our man makes now
is not match to cigarette
but the screen of a phone which he checks and taps,
the blue dot on a satellite map moving on foot
onwards from one bleak mood to this –
Feels a little fresh, he says
to no-one but himself
under his breath, a release.

TREE

The tree wasn't planted the usual way,
by councillors, there was no plaque
in memory of the deceased,
but you should have seen it grow.
The limbs cut back for buses
soon reached over the traffic,
the roots undermining the ring road.
Nobody questioned the tree
dwarfing their town, overshadowing
the Millennium municipal buildings
or drew a connection between it
and the outsize insects and birds.

Some saw magic among the branches,
an eye looking down on them, a few
spotted a naked woman lolling in the leaves.
Most complained of the sun
blotted out or the pain in their necks
from looking up, so no-one noticed
the tower block down the road
transforming itself into an immense cabinet,
the multi-storey turning into a table,
then the coat laid over it,
as if someone had arrived
and was calling this home.

RICH

What, I ask, *is doing that*
on the ceiling? I could guess
light messing with a glass but wanted a fresh miracle –
alien communication, upset spirits arguing, until now
undiscovered insect? Or delicately winged
23rd century time-travelling machine
that lands on the bookshelf then fidgets?
Or intricate thin-stringed instrument
in miniature, mounted on the wall
and strummed by human breath?
Of course not. Only the everyday
accidental collaboration, glass half-full
lets light meet water and indicates
how rich we are – there's sunlight,
here's drink and somewhere
to sit and you're alive. Or *Just my cup* you say
and jog the table again.

THE HONEY LIGHT

A good day not to wake up, says Anthony.
Wes, the driver of the truck, grunts agreement
or annoyance. But if he did comment now,
he would say how he loves the aftertaste
of his egg breakfast with the strong tea.
Anthony drops from the cab, lumbers towards
the car park at the back of the Red Herring.
He levers the bin up, starts wheeling back
and it's here a colour runs through his mind.
The light in Famona Road in August? Or the light
between Jubilee Terrace and the George Borrow
down by the railway line, on a Saturday, late.
He's with his old man, the football scores done with,
the radio clicked off. They've been stuck
as a train goes through. Now the cars start up
and, as they slowly reach the track and judder over,
(his dad a careful driver, not wanting to risk
the suspension) there's a flash of honey light
that washes over their windscreen. Take a snapshot
and you would see father and son creasing their eyes.
Something honks, he thinks, as he flips
open the lid of the bin on last week's fish.

THERE ARE DAYS

when what you thought was trapped
filling the kitchen with desperate chirps
from behind the air vent, forces you
up the stepladder, reluctantly
to prise and remove the plastic
from the wall to reveal
a nest you quickly leave
undisturbed, retreat
replacing the four screws and outside
you are delighted to locate the bird
that fidgets on the gutter before
it drops down again
and again you watch –
there's a pair – every minute one
or the other returns with a beakful.

And there are mornings
when the herring gull arrives
and waits for its moment.

ON TAKING THE SALAD BOWL

with both hands, well held
then cradled
to my chest, gathered
by the goalkeeper
I never really was, I remember
the white-haired man
on the street, umbrella swung
into bat, that fast delivery
finally returned
from forty years back,
all within three steps.

REVERSING

It leans on me heavy
this leaving, Sunday evening
her, no dog
street lights
that soon switch off.

I stay longer, it's often ten
I still park up the drive
but as I reverse
she follows slowly
to close the gate behind me.

It's always night and late
but before I pull away, I stop –
not to miss the wave
to see her safely up the step
until I guess the door is locked.

LATE FOR MY OWN FUNERAL

Just like my mother said, I knew
I'd never be ready, the mourners kept waiting –
dark coats and steaming breath,
fingers to watches like pulses. I've no excuse –
best not blame roadworks when I was
only ever faffing around, foolish,
another novel started I can't hope to finish,
asking myself *why* do I have to
fit the Hoover bag before I finally leave
when I should be arriving, never allowing
enough time until I'm breathless
not moving in all this traffic,
beyond stress with no signal,
unable even to text
Please start without me.

IN LINE

Waiting what seems like forever
for chips to fry, he sees himself
all the way down the line.

Just a boy
with a fist of coins,
eye level to the counter.

Jack the lad,
ordering for two, hungry
for the evening ahead.

The family man with complications,
two large portions, three small, two with fish
but one without, always without something.

Then, retired,
knowing what to expect,
wrapped up in yesterday's news.

What happens next? Somebody pays
and we all move one step forward, catching
the draught from the door as they go.

MAN CYCLING MADLY DOWN A HILL
After the painting by Mary Newcomb

For once, he was not late, no chicken charring in the oven
He was not trying to make it back before dark without lights

There was no early kick-off to catch (only the Europa League)
He was not out of condition, this was nowhere near top speed

He had not just remembered the place he had left his phone
He was not busting a gut to get to the shop before it shut

There was no chip-pan fire, no lifeboat to be launched
No dash for the post or sudden rush to confess before she went

He was not avoiding the man next door who wanted a word
Not worried about the old bloke on the bike behind pedalling fast

He was not attempting to beat his best time to Bennett's corner
(8 minutes 22 seconds), not hurrying at the first fat drops of rain

His performance was not drug enhanced or wind assisted
This was not him picking up the pace to shake off a loopy wasp

He was cycling madly simply because he likes it this quick
And for every lovely downhill there'll be the struggle up.

LIST OF SUBSCRIBERS

Neil Astley
Anne Berkeley
Rasik Bhadresa
Simon Brod
Marjorie Carter
Elizabeth Cook
C M Daventry
Robert Delahunty
Emily Dening
David Edwards
Robert Etty
James Flynn
Richard Furniss
Charlotte Gann
Elizabeth Glodek
Lydia Harris
Emma Hellyer
Ramona Herdman
Elizabeth Horsley
Matt Howard
Colin Hughes
Keith Hutson
Bill Jackson
Luke Kennard
Dore Kiesselbach
Fiona Larkin
Gill Learner
Jo Leverett
Rob Lock
Chris McCabe
Gemma Mills McGrath
Ian McMillan
Lydia Macpherson
Lorraine Mariner
Marcia Menter

Helen Mitchell
Kim Moore
Helena Nelson
Sean O'Connor
Stephen Payne
Beverly Payton
Alesha Racine
Simon Ratcliffe
Ann & Peter Sansom
Ann Stewart
Alicia Stubbersfield
Lizzi Thistlethwayte
Pam Thompson
Ann Thwaite
Edward Vanderpump
John Vaughan
Roger Waterfield
Derek Webster
John Williams
Jackie Wills
Anthony Wilson
Frances Wilson
Helen Jagger Wood
Sarah Wright
Luke Samuel Yates

And others who wish to remain anonymous